Faithful God: : Testimonies of Healing

Written by Jan Asleson
Illustrated/Designs Layout by Jan Asleson

Copyright © 2024 Jan Asleson

All Rights reserved. No part of this book may be reproduced in any form or by any electronic or mechanical means including information storage and retrieval systems, without permission in writing from the publisher, except by reviewers, who may quote brief passages in review.

ISBN 9798218529321

KJV: Scripture quotations marked KJV are taken from the King James Version. Public domain.

Printed in the United States of America by Ingram/Spark Lightning Source

Published by Spirit Wings Designs 2024
daslpacker55@yahoocom

Faithful God Testimonies of Healing

Created By
Jan Asleson

This book is dedicated to:

My Heavenly Father
the Great I AM
Almighty God
He who holds all
my tears in
His Bottle

Foreword

"And they overcame him by the blood of the Lamb, and by the word of their testimony; and they loved not their lives unto the death." (Revelation 12:11 KJV).

What is a testimony? It is a declaration of an event that is backed by evidence, by proof. This little book focuses on supernatural healings from God. Each story came at a time when I could not help myself.

Not only have I experienced healings for myself but also for animals in my care. A good definition of healing is: To make free from injury or disease, to restore, to correct.

"But unto you that fear my name shall the Son of righteousness arise with healing in his wings." (Malachi 4:2 KJV).

Please consider, in no way am I anymore special than anyone else. I do believe that the Heavenly Father takes care of His children, in His way and His time. I certainly don't have all the answers! Some are called to their eternal home, experiencing complete healing. I have dear friends who are trusting God for healing and are standing in faith for that to manifest in their lives. I am not the judge! There are many scriptures in God's word about healing. I choose to believe His word and take it to heart. Am I walking in total healing? No! Yet, I trust my Father God to:

"For it is God which worketh in you both to will and to do of His good pleasure." (Philippians 2:13 KJV).

My hope and purpose for this book is to encourage you, the reader, to discover God the Healer. Not just physical healing but spiritual, emotional, and relational; healing in every area of your life. I'm not talking about just information and knowledge of God, but a personal relationship with Him. The testimonies relate to physical healings. Some healings happen instantaneously, others over a period of time. I have experienced both. The following scriptures have helped me tremendously in my times of waiting on the Lord for His merciful Healing.

"No weapon formed against thee shall prosper; and every tongue that shall rise against thee in judgement thou shalt condemn. This is the heritage of the servants of the Lord and their righteousness is of me, saith the Lord." (Isaiah 54:17 KJV).

"Many are the afflictions of the righteous: but the Lord delivereth him out of them all." (Psalm 34:19 KJV).

"Praise the Lord, my soul, and forget not all His benefits - who forgives all your sins and heals all your diseases." (Psalm 103:2-3 KJV).

"So do not fear for I am with you; do not be dismayed, for I am your God. I will strengthen you and help you; I will uphold thee with the right hand of my righteousness." (Isaiah 41:10 KJV).

HEALING ONE

Much to my surprise I was diagnosed with Lyme's disease the summer of 1991. I had not felt well for some time. I was 34 at the time and was athletic and was running 9 miles 5-6 days a week. Eventually I was not able to run. I was stubborn though and had refused to go to the doctor. I was always pushing myself, always busy, never slowed down. Before I became ill my husband David and I went to a Christian conference in the next state. I went up for prayer at some point to see if I could get "a Word from God." It was a prayer line, and a man came and stood before me and started to pray. He then began to ask God to "heal me." I blurted out, "I'm not sick!" He got a confused look on his face, and said he'd pray again. Once again, he prayed that God would heal me. At that point I thanked him for his prayer and left, thinking that he really missed it. Well, he didn't miss it…it was a couple months later that I began to feel exhausted and was not able to do much. I couldn't walk up the stairs and was having neurological problems. I hurt all over. I eventually went to see the local PA. In the early 90's Lyme's disease was difficult to diagnose because the bacteria would hide and the tests were often ineffective. The PA I saw had the year before mis-diagnosed a patient with the disease and they had almost died. He put me on a 2 month round of antibiotics and sent me home. Later that day as I was sitting in a rocking chair talking to the Lord about why I was in the predicament I found myself in, I heard Him say to me "I will heal you if you will rest in me." "Huh?" I had no idea what He was talking about! But, I learned what that meant as I spent day after day sitting in a rocking chair meditating on what resting in Him meant. My recovery took almost 2 years, which was a major challenge for a "Let's get things done" person like myself. The medical community says that the Lyme's bacteria never leaves your body. I did fully recover and many years later was tested multiple times but the disease was gone. Through the healing process I learned a valuable lesson of Resting in God. Physical rest and relaxation are also important as constant stress and the pressure of "push push push" can lower your immune system. Because I tended to be a perfectionist and a pleaser of man, I believe I was vulnerable when the tick came along and bit me. Yet Father God in His Mercy and Compassion delivered me.

"The Lord is gracious, and full of compassion; slow to anger, and of great mercy." (Psalm 145:8 KJV).

HEALING TWO

Cancer, the word that strikes fear in the hearts of many. March 2009 I was diagnosed with a rare, aggressive ovarian cancer. I had not been feeling well. I made an appointment with a GP doctor. The morning of the appointment while spending time with the Lord, the Father spoke to me and said, "Read Psalm 91." I did. He said, "Speak it over yourself." I did. I even printed it out and put it in my purse. During the exam the doctor felt something abnormal in my pelvic area. He thought it was a cyst and would be easy to remove. An appointment for surgery was made. That night I experienced intense abdominal pain to the point that I went to the emergency room. They scheduled a sonogram for the next day. They saw a mass and I was admitted to the hospital because it was cutting off my intestines. It was my 51st birthday, having a wonderful time in the OBGYN ward waiting for surgery the next day. During my time waiting for my surgery the next morning I had total peace as I meditated on Psalm 91. Early in the morning of the surgery, around 5:00 am I was listening to worship music on my laptop and I had a vision. I saw Father God stand up off His throne. He walked into the surgery theatre with His right arm extended and He said to me, "I will not allow the enemy to take you, you will come home when I call you home." That filled me with such Assurance, such Joy! I was wheeled into surgery. When I woke up from surgery I heard the two doctors say that they thought I had a fighting chance. They had taken the cancerous tumor out and cleaned my insides up the best they could. My head was reeling! How could this happen to me! Of course they wanted me to do chemo, but I wanted a second opinion. I went to MD Anderson and was given the same diagnosis and treatment. I resisted the idea of chemo and went on a raw food diet, juicing fruits and vegetables, for four months. During that time my intestines kinked three times and I ended up back in the hospital on an IV drip along with a cat scan for a few days. Once again I felt ill like I had at first. The cancer had come back and wrapped around my small intestine, yet overall I continued to have peace. I was sent to another hospital where the oncologist surgeon specialized in ovarian cancer. The surgery lasted hours and they took eight inches of my small intestine. I was in the hospital two weeks. I experienced a difficult recovery. I decided to do the chemo, but I was so weak they had to administer a blood transfusion in order for my strength to come back. When I went in for my first chemo, within seconds I went into anaphylaxis shock. I saw black and was passing out while the head nurse was shouting my name. My blood pressure was 30 over 15. While they were wheeling me to the emergency room I was saying the name of Jesus over and over again. I even thought that maybe I'd die and go to heaven and come back with an amazing testimony. They gave me a shot of adrenaline to get my blood pressure back up and I went into shock. I was in ICU for a couple of nights, then sent back home to recover once again. A couple of weeks later I started chemo. Because they had changed the medication I was able to handle the injection which lasted several hours. The poison didn't hit me till the second day and I felt like I had been run over by a truck. I laid in bed for several days, sleep was the only reprieve. Once I was able to get up I was able to manage till the next round of chemo. At that point I began to question my faith. Because I had come to the Lord during the faith movement, in other words, if you had enough faith you would never get sick, be poor or experience any other major tribulation, I thought surely I had fallen short in my faith. Faith seemed like a mystical word to me, how did it come, how did you get it? Long story short, Trusting God no matter what helped me to discover faith. The Lord even told me "Don't fear being fearful, don't let it paralyze you".

The doctors wanted me to do 6 rounds of chemo, but because the injections were so destructive to my body, I decided to only do four, after much prayer and confirmation. During the whole journey I also did holistic treatments so that my body would heal. An amazing holistic doctor named Karen was part of God's plan to deliver me from the cancer. She is now one of my closest friends. I have been asked, 'if you had faith why did you do chemo'? And, 'because you did chemo, God didn't heal you'. When I was first diagnosed with the cancer I was Stage one. After the second surgery I was Stage three. I was told that only five percent of women that have that type of cancer survive. God told me that He would deliver me and heal me and He did. It was not an instantaneous healing yet still a healing. During my journey God also healed me of emotional trauma. I had a lot of self hatred because of wrong choices I had made in the past, and also difficult family relationships.

I chose to forgive myself and others, and also to forgive God. He had not done anything wrong but my perspective from my heart and pain had blinded me. This year, 2004, I have been cancer free for fifteen years. Praise God!

"He that dwelleth in the secret place of the most High shall abide under the shadow of the Almighty. I will say of the Lord, He is my refuge and my fortress; my God; in Him will I trust. Surely He will deliver thee from the snare of the fowler, and from the noisome pestilence. He shall cover thee with His feathers, and under His wings shalt thou trust: His truth shall be thy shield and buckler. Thou shalt not be afraid for the terror by night; nor for the arrow that flieth by day; Nor for the pestilence that walketh in darkness; nor for the destruction that wasteth at noonday. A thousand shall fall by thy side, and ten thousand at thy right hand; but it shall not come nigh thee. Only with thy eyes shalt thou behold and see

the reward of the wicked. Because thou hast made the Lord, which is my refuge, even the most high, thy habitation; There shall no evil befall thee, neither shall any plague come nigh thy dwelling. For He shall give His angels charge over thee, to keep thee in all thy ways. They shall bear thee up in their hands, lest thou dash thy foot against a stone. Thou shalt tread upon the lion and adder: the young lion and the dragon shalt though trample under feet. Because He hath set His love upon me, therefore will I deliver him: I will set him on high, because he hath known my name. He shall call upon me, and I will answer him: I will be with him in trouble; I will deliver him and honour him. With long life I will satisfy him and show him my salvation. (Psalm 91 KJV).

HEALING THREE

For many years I took care of my elderly father. We lived out in the country on 80 wooded acres. Me and my husband lived in a small dwelling called The Cabin. It was a quarter of a mile from my Dad's house through the woods, or a half a mile if we drove. A typical day would include me walking over to his house morning and evening, having coffee with him and taking care of his needs. I also fed my two horses and walked my dog morning and evening. My husband was often away from home with his job. My daughter lived in the area but worked during the day. One morning as I stepped off my porch step I twisted my ankle. It was so bad I could barely walk. I managed to get all my chores done, including taking care of Dad. By the time I got back home I was in great pain. I called and made an appointment with my PA, got in quick and did an Xray. My ankle wasn't broken but severely sprained. His order to me was "Stay off it!"

"Yeah right", I grumbled as I hobbled into the cabin. Even walking with a cane was challenging. That night as I lay in bed talking to my Father God, I cried out to Him for His Mercy and Grace. I told Him of my need to be mobile so I could take care of all my responsibilities. I told Him that I trusted Him to meet my needs. The next morning when I woke up my ankle didn't hurt. I got out of bed and stood up, No pain; No swelling! Totally healed as if I'd never sprained it! Praises rang through the cabin that morning.

Two years later I experienced the same thing all over again. I didn't bother going to the PA but cried out to the Lord again for His help. Again, I went to bed thanking and trusting Him. I woke up the next morning totally healed.

"But my God shall supply all your need according to His riches in glory by Christ Jesus." (Philippians 4:19 KJV)

HEALING FOUR

God has put in my heart a love for animals. I see many animals, birds, and wildlife on the 80 acres of woods where we live. One morning as I stepped outside I saw a fallen dove on the ground. It looked as if its neck was broken. Many times birds hit the windows of the house and are killed. I picked the dove up, saddened. It was limp, its eyes dead. As I held it in my hands I cried out to God to revive it, while holding it and caressing it. In a moment it came back to life and flew off. Because the dove was on the property that I managed I felt a sense of responsibility.

"A righteous man regardeth the life of his beast...." (Proverbs 12:10 KJV)

Healing Five

The last healing testimony I want to share in this little book is about an Arabian horse I had. She was 23 at the time and she was the "Alpha" horse. She was also the watch horse and was always aware of potential danger in the woods or something new. Her name was Dawn. I had two other horses at the time, both Arabians. Dawn was always pushing the gelding around and would even become mean to him at times. One morning I went out to feed them and she was in bad shape. Roles had reversed and Starbuck, the gelding was now the Alpha. He was tormenting her and I had to separate them. When the veterinary came out she did a sonogram of Dawn's right hip and said that it was broken. We would need to put her down. I stood there with my arms around her and once again cried out to God to heal her, hopeful of His love and mercy. Before my very eyes He healed her. He said to me

"Because you love her so much I will heal her, because I love you."

Jan Asleson —Author-Artist— Publisher

Jan Loves to encourage others to pursue and discover the God and Father of Abraham, Isaac and Jacob. Creativity is her forte. She has won awards for her work and loves sharing her creations with others. She is skilled in portraiture, Acrylics, Pastels, and Watercolor. She imprints her art on natural fibers and is a Professional Jeweler creating one of a kind pieces in gold and silver with precious and semi-precious stones.

Jan is married to David and lives in Southeast KS in the woods.

You may contact her at:

daslpacker55@yahoo.com

www.ingramcontent.com/pod-product-compliance
Lightning Source LLC
LaVergne TN
LVHW061049070526
838201LV00074B/5241